AMOR ET AMICITIA

Part of a marble sarcophagus representing a married couple and attendants. From Rome. Sc. 2307, A. H. Smith, *A Catalogue of Sculpture in the Department of Greek and Roman Antiquities, British Museum*, Vols. I-III (1896-1904). (London, British Museum)

THEMES IN LATIN LITERATURE

amor et amicitia
imperium et civitas
urbs antiqua

AMOR ET AMICITIA

A COLLECTION OF LATIN POEMS, LETTERS, AND EPITAPHS
WITH VOCABULARY, NOTES, AND QUESTIONS

COMPILED AND EDITED BY PATRICIA E. BELL

CAMBRIDGE
UNIVERSITY PRESS

PUBLISHED BY THE PRESS SYNDICATE OF THE UNIVERSITY OF CAMBRIDGE
The Pitt Building, Trumpington Street, Cambridge CB2 1RP, United Kingdom

CAMBRIDGE UNIVERSITY PRESS
The Edinburgh Building, Cambridge CB2 2RU, United Kingdom
40 West 20th Street, New York, NY 10011-4211, USA
10 Stamford Road, Oakleigh, Melbourne 3166, Australia

First published 1988 by Irwin Publishing Inc., Canada
This edition first published 1989
Fifth printing 1997

Printed in the United Kingdom by Woolnough Bookbinding Limited
Irthlingborough, Northants

A catalogue record for this book is available from the British Library

Library of Congress cataloguing-in-publication data

Amor et amicitia: a collection of latin poems, letters and epitaphs
  with vocabulary, notes and questions/compiled and edited by
  Patricia E. Bell.
  1. Latin language — Readers. 2 Love — Literary collections.
  3. Family — Literary collections. 4. Friendship — Literary
  collections. I. Bell, Patricia E.
  PA2095.A46 1988
  478.6'421 — dc19

ISBN 0 521 37736 6

Cover photograph: Part of a marble sarcophagus representing a married couple and attendants.
From Rome. Sc. 2307, A.H. Smith, *A Catalogue of Sculpture in the Department of Greek and
Roman Antiquities, British Museum*, Vols. I-III (1896-1904).

Table of Contents

LOVERS

FAMILY

FRIENDS

PLACES

I dedicate this book to my husband, my daughter, and my students. Their indulgence for my love of teaching Latin made this collection possible.

NOTE TO THE TEACHER

This text is designed to provide you with readings suitable for students beginning to read original Latin. The Latin of all the selections is either unadapted or is only very mildly edited. What editing there is takes the form of deletion rather than that of alteration.

Over 400 lines are offered here for an investigation of the theme of *amor et amicitia*. Additional readings for the further pursuit of each aspect of the theme are given at the end of each subtopic.

Since each selection is a self-contained unit with its own notes and vocabulary, there is no need to read every selection. Nor is it necessary to read the selections in the order given here.

The discussion questions at the end of each subtopic are intended to be directional, not comprehensive, and can readily be adapted to suit whatever selections you have chosen to read.

TO THE STUDENT

For convenience of discussion and comparison, the selections in this text have been organized according to subtopics of the theme of *amor et amicitia*. The letters, epitaphs, and poetry reveal Roman attitudes to love and friendship in its varying facets: love for wives, lovers, family, friends, and places.

Notes and vocabulary have been included to assist you in your translating of each selection. Since sound and rhythm are important in both prose and poetry, you should read all selections aloud not only at the beginning of your study, but also at the conclusion of your analysis and discussion. In this way, you should be able to impart to your second reading all your new understanding of the passage.

The Initial Questions at the end of each section are intended to highlight only certain aspects of each passage. They should lead you into detailed analysis of the writer's treatment of the theme. They should not predetermine or limit your own exploration or the class discussion. You are expected to quote the Latin words and phrases that support your conclusions for every question.

The Discussion Questions are more general. They are designed to help you assess the distinctiveness of each writer's artistic conception of the theme, to form conclusions about the similarities and differences in approach of the different writers, and to explore and assess the effectiveness of the Roman expression of the theme.

GLOSSARY OF SOME LITERARY TERMS USED IN *THEMES IN LATIN LITERATURE*

In writing a literary appreciation for a piece of literature, it is not enough simply to list literary devices and examples. Always examine critically each device to see *how* the writer uses it and *what* effect is achieved by its use in that context.

anaphora: the repetition of an important word at the beginning of several successive clauses

alliteration: the repetition of the same sound, usually a consonant, at the beginning of two or more adjacent words

antithesis: a rhetorical contrast achieved by the balanced or parallel arrangement of words, clauses, or sentences with a strong contrast in meaning

assonance: the repetition of the same vowel sounds in two or more adjacent words

asyndeton: the omission of conjunctions or customary connecting words

atmosphere: the mood pervading the literary work

cadence: a measured rhythmic sequence or flow of words in prose or poetry

connotation: the cluster of implicit or associated meanings of a word as distinguished from that word's denotative or specific meaning

diction: the deliberate choice of words

ellipsis: the omission of word(s) necessary for the grammatical structure of a sentence

emphatic word order:

  (i) **chiasmus**: a criss-cross arrangement usually resulting from the separation of two nouns and the adjectives that modify each

  (ii) **first and last word positions**: placing an important word at these emphatic positions in a line of poetry

  (iii) **framing**: a word placed out of its usual order and "framed" by a pair of related words to make the word stand out prominently

  (iv) **interlocking word order**: the words of one noun-adjective phrase alternating with those of another

  (v) **juxtaposition**: two words or phrases set side by side to intensify meaning

  (vi) **separation**: separating grammatically related words (e.g., noun—noun, noun—adjective) to produce a word picture of the meaning conveyed by the words

epic: a long narrative poem in elevated style, typically having as its subject a hero on whose exploits depends to some degree the fate of a nation or race

epic simile: a comparison extended beyond the obvious comparison by further details

epigram: a brief and pointed poem, usually ending with a surprising or witty turn of thought

figurative language: language that departs from the literal standard meaning in order to achieve a special effect, e.g., metaphor, personification, simile

genre: a literary form, e.g., epic, lyric, satire

hyperbole: an extravagant exaggeration of fact used to express strong feeling and not intended to be taken literally

imagery: the poetic technique of making mental pictures in such a way as to make the emotion or mood appeal vividly to the reader and to produce a clue to poetic intent

interjection: a sudden phrase or word that interrupts the grammatical progress of the sentence

irony: the use of words that convey a sense or attitude contrary to what is literally expressed; e.g., often ostensible praise or approval implies condemnation or contempt

metaphor: an indirect comparison whereby one thing is compared to another without the expressed indication of the point of similarity

mythological allusion: a brief reference to mythological details the writer assumes will be readily recognized by the reader instead of stating directly the myth or name of the person or thing

onomatopoeia or imitative harmony: the use of a word whose sound resembles the sound it describes

oxymoron: a rhetorical contrast achieved by putting together two contradictory terms

paradox: a statement that seems contradictory but that reveals a coherent truth

parallelism or balanced structure: the recurrence or repetition of a grammatical pattern

pathos: the creation of pity or sorrow in the reader

periodic sentence: a sentence designed to arouse interest and suspense by keeping the meaning unclear until the very end

personification: the description of an inanimate object or concept in terms of human qualities

rhetoric: the presentation of ideas in a persuasive manner, usually used for effectiveness in oratory or public speaking; for specific rhetoric devices, see anaphora, alliteration, etc.

rhetorical question: a question used for its persuasive effect and for which no answer is expected or for which the answer is self-evident; it is used to achieve rhetorical emphasis stronger than a direct statement

rhythm: the pattern of long and short syllables in each line of poetry

rhyme: the repetition of the same sound at the end of two or more words

satire: a literary form in which prevailing vices or follies are held up to humour and ridicule and evoke towards them attitudes of amusement, indignation, or contempt

simile: a stated comparison often indicated by a term such as *velut*, *similis*, or *qualis*. A simile extended to embellish, complete, or reinforce the narrative with a vivid picture, the details of which are not always relevant to the original point of comparison, is called an **epic simile**.

theme: the central or dominating idea of a literary work

tone: the attitude of the writer to the subject. The tone may be characterized, for example, as formal or informal, solemn or playful, satirical, serious, or ironic.

transferred epithet: the application of a significant modifier to a word other than the one to which it actually belongs

vivid particularization: a concrete or specified description, usually achieved by the use of proper nouns rich in connotations

SHORT BIOGRAPHIES OF LATIN AUTHORS QUOTED IN AMOR ET AMICITIA

Catullus: Poet (C.84 B.C.—C. 54 B.C.)

Quintus Valerius Catullus was born in Verona, a town in northern Italy. Very little is known of his life, but it appears that his family was fairly wealthy. Catullus came to Rome c. 62 B.C. and entered fashionable literary society where he met and fell in love with Clodia whom he addressed in his poetry as "Lesbia." Their turbulent love affair inspired many of his poems. In 57 B.C., Catullus travelled to Asia Minor with the new governor, Gaius Memmius. While there, he visited the tomb of his brother who was buried near Troy and composed his famous elegy on his brother's death. The date of Catullus' death is not known, but it seems that he died about the age of thirty.

Catullus' poems are varied in subject and tone, and he established in Latin literature a place for simple, light, occasional verse. In his love poetry, he seems the most modern of Latin poets because of his frank exploration of the emotions.

Cicero; Orator, Statesman, Philosopher, Letter Writer (106 B.C.—43 B.C.)

Marcus Tullius Cicero was born in Arpinum, southeast of Rome, of a family of equestrian rank. He studied rhetoric and philosophy in Rome. Although a *novus homo*, he advanced politically, even to positions usually reserved for patricians, because of his success as a lawyer. He was particularly respected because of his prosecution of Verres in 70 B.C. when he defeated the leading orator of the day, Quintus Hortensius. About 79 B.C., he married Terentia. He was acclaimed *pater patriae* in 63 B.C., when as consul he discovered and frustrated a revolutionary conspiracy led by Lucius Sergius Catilina. About 59 B.C., it appears that Gaius Julius Caesar attempted to win Cicero's approval of the newly formed (First) Triumvirate. However, Cicero refused to condone the unconstitutional nature of that governing group. Almost immediately the government passed a bill sending into exile anyone who had executed Romans without allowing an appeal. This bill was directed against Cicero who, as consul, had had the Catilinarian conspirators executed. A bitterly disillusioned Cicero left Italy in 58 B.C., but he was pardoned and recalled in 57 B.C. In 51 B.C., he was sent as governor to the province of Cilicia in Asia Minor. He returned to Italy to discover that Julius Caesar and Gnaeus Pompeius Magnus (Pompey the Great) had quarrelled, dissolving the First Triumvirate, and that civil war was imminent. After a period of confusion, Cicero made the agonizing decision to support Pompey. Although Pompey was defeated by Caesar, Caesar pardoned Cicero in 47 B.C. In 46 B.C., Cicero divorced his wife Terentia. The following year, his beloved daughter died. After the assassination of

Caesar in 44 B.C., Cicero, hoping for a restoration of the old traditional republican order, began to denounce Marcus Antonius as the man who had tried to make Caesar a king. Unfortunately for Cicero, the Second Triumvirate was formed by Antony and Octavian (Caesar's heir and later known as Augustus), and Lepidus. With Octavian's reluctant consent, Cicero's name was put on the proscription list. Cicero was murdered by Antony's soldiers in 43 B.C.

Politically, Cicero was a moderate opposed to revolution and change. He was bewildered and confused by the political unrest in which he lived and he found it difficult to be decisive or consistent in the political dilemmas that faced him. However, his strengths in oratory, political theory, philosophy, and literary criticism made an incomparable impression on his own time and on subsequent European thought and literary style. Over 300 of his letters to family and friends survive, giving us an invaluable picture of both the man and this turbulent period of Roman history.

Horace: Poet (65 B.C.—8 B.C.)

Quintus Horatius Flaccus, born in Venusia in southern Italy, was the son of a freedman who contrived to give Horace the best education attainable both in Rome and in Athens. Horace served for some years as a clerk in the civil service in Rome while he wrote poetry. About 38 B.C., Horace was introduced by the poet Vergil to Maecenas who became Horace's patron. Maecenas in turn introduced Horace to the emperor Augustus and the Augustan poets, and gave to Horace the Sabine Farm outside Rome which became Horace's beloved refuge from Rome. In 17 B.C., Horace was asked to write an official hymn celebrating ten years of peace under Augustus. In this way, Horace was openly recognized as the foremost lyric poet of Rome.

Horace's reputation lies mainly in his *Odes*, in which he adapted the traditional Greek lyric metres to the Latin language. The first three books of the *Odes* were composed between 33 B.C. and 23 B.C. The final book appeared about 15 B.C. Horace's poetry is characterized by unsurpassed technical mastery of language and metre. His polished verses with compressed and allusive use of language are the result of painstaking effort. His poems reveal a simple, sincere, friendly man of many interests. He is patriotic, good humoured, and tolerant. Unlike Catullus, Horace is not the passionate participant in life but the amused onlooker.

Martial: Epigrammatist (C. A.D. 40—A.D. 103)

Marcus Valerius Martialis, of Spanish birth, came to Rome c. A.D. 64. Little is known of his life apart from his twelve books of epigrams (short, pointed, or satirical poems on contemporary subjects). Apparently he was poor and lived in an apartment house in Rome, but he later owned a small farm at Nomentum, northeast of Rome. He depended on the favour of various patrons while he wrote poetry. About A.D. 98, he retired to Spain to a property given him by a patron. He died in Spain.

His poems, of which more than 1500 survive, provide realistic glimpses of the varied details of everyday life. Martial is a witty observer of people. He does not moralize, but rather maintains an amused, tolerant attitude towards the human vices he exposes. The unexpected twist with which he ends many of his epigrams has become a standard feature of the genre.

Pliny the Younger: Letter Writer, Statesman (C. A.D. 61-C. A.D. 112)

Gaius Plinius Caecilius Secundus was born of the artistocracy of Comum, a lakeside town in northern Italy. He was adopted by his uncle, Pliny the Elder. At Rome, Pliny studied law, oratory, and philosophy. He rose steadily up the *cursus honorum* (the regular steps of the political ladder), becoming consul in A.D. 100 and then curator of the Tiber and its banks. About A.D. 110, he was sent, by special appointment by the emperor Trajan, to govern the Roman province of Bithynia in Asia Minor. He was to investigate and settle the unrest there. Pliny was married three times. His third marriage, to Calpurnia, was a very happy one.

Although he was a distinguished lawyer, only one of Pliny's speeches survives. However, over 200 of his letters survive and with them a vast quantity of useful information about the way of life during the first century A.D. His correspondence with Trajan provides a valuable picture of the administration of an imperial province. His style is characterized by his brevity, simplicity, and frankness as well as by a touch of a self-consciously literary style.

WIVES

A sixth-century B.C. sarcophagus showing an affectionate Etruscan husband and wife. (Rome, Museo Nazionale di Villa Giulia)

PLINY WRITES ABOUT HIS WIFE

C. PLINIUS CALPURNIAE HISPULLAE SUAE S.

cum sis pietatis exemplum, fratremque amantissimum
dilexeris, filiam eius ut tuam diligis; nec tantum amitae
ei adfectumque verum etiam patris amissi repraesen-
tas. non dubito maximo tibi gaudio fore, cum   5
cognoveris dignam patre, dignam te, dignam avo
evadere. summum est acumen, summa frugalitas; amat
me, quod castitatis indicium est. accedit his studium
litterarum, quod ex mei caritate concepit. meos libellos
habet, lectitat, ediscit etiam. quam sollicita est cum   10
ego acturus sum! quanto cum egi gaudio adficitur!
disponit qui nuntient sibi quos clamores excitarim,
quem eventum iudicii tulerim.

   eadem, si quando recito, in proximo discreta velo,
sedet. laudesque nostras avidissimis auribus excipit.   15
versus meos cantat etiam formatque cithara. non artifice aliquo docente, sed amor, qui est magister optimus.

   his ex causis in spem certissimam adducor,
perpetuam nobis maioremque in dies futuram esse con-
cordiam. non enim aetatem meam aut corpus, quae   20
paulatim occidunt ac senescunt, sed gloriam diligit.
nec aliud decet puellam tuis manibus educatam, tuis
praeceptis institutam. nihil in conturbernio tuo vidit
nisi sanctum honestumque; et me amare ex tua
praedicatione consuevit. certatim ergo tibi gratias   25
agimus, ego quod illam mihi, illa quod me sibi dederis.
vale.

PLINY, *EPISTULAE* IV.19

Pliny Writes About His Wife

Pliny writes to Calpurnia Hispulla, his wife's aunt, to express his gratitude for his wife's many virtues.

C. = *Gaius*
S. = *salutem dat* sends greetings
pietas, tatis, f family affection
amantissimus, a, um devoted
diligo, ere, lexi love
nec tantum...verum etiam not only...but also
amita, ae, f aunt
*adfectus, us, m affection, feeling
amissus, a, um lost, dead
repraesento, are show, display
5 *non dubito* I don't doubt that
maximo tibi gaudio fore it will be a great
   pleasure to you
cognosco, ere, cognovi learn, discover:
   completed here by acc. + inf. *(eam) evadere*
dignus, a, um + abl. worthy
avus, i, m grandfather
evado, ere turn out
acumen, minis, n common sense
frugalitas, tatis, f thrift
castitas, tatis, f virtue
indicium, i, n sign
accedit his in addition to these (virtues)
studium, i, n enthusiasm
litterae, arum, f. pl. literature
caritas, atis, f fondness
concipio, ere, cepi develop, take up
libellus, i, m book
10 *lectito, are* read over and over again
edisco, ere learn by heart
sollicitus, a, um concerned, worried
acturus about to speak in court
quanto...gaudio with what joy
egi (from ago, agere, egi) I have finished
   (i.e., speaking in court)
adficio, ere affect
dispono, ere arrange for
qui nuntient sibi: rel. cl. of purpose people to
   tell her
excitarim = excitaverim: excito, are rouse

eventus, us, m result, verdict
iudicium, i, n case, trial
fero, ferre, tuli get, win
si quando whenever
in proximo in the next room
discretus, a, um separated
velum, i, n curtain
15 *laus, laudis, f* praise
nostras = meas
avidus, a, um eager
auris, is, f ear
excipio, ere receive, catch
formo, are accompany
cithara, ae, f lute
non artifice aliquo docente: abl. abs. she is
   taught not by some other musician
artifex, ficis, m musician
spes, spei, f hope, expectation
adducor I am persuaded, convinced
maior, maius greater
in dies from day to day
concordia, ae, f harmony
20 *aetas, tatis, f* age
paulatim gradually
occido, ere die, decay
senesco, ere grow old
gloria, ae, f fame, distinction
nec aliud decet (puellam) nor is anything else
   fitting for a girl
educatus, a, um educated
praeceptum, i, n guidance, teaching
institutus, a, um trained
contubernium, i, n household
nisi except
sanctus, a, um pure
25 *praedicatio, onis, f* praise, commendation
consuesco, ere become accustomed
certatim in eager rivalry
ergo therefore

3

Two Epitaphs on Wives

An Epitaph on Claudia

hospes, quod deico paullum est; asta ac pellege.
heic est sepulcrum hau pulcrum pulcrai feminae:
nomen parentes nominarunt Claudiam.
suom mareitum corde deilexit souo:
gnatos duos creavit: horunc alterum   5
in terra linquit, alium sub terra locat.
sermone lepido, tum autem incessu commodo,
domum servavit. lanam fecit. dixi, abei.

CORPUS INSCRIPTIONUM LATINARUM I.2 1211

An Epitaph on Aurelia

Lucius Aurelius Lucii libertus Hermia lanius
   de colle Viminali.
haec quae me fato praecessit, corpore casto
   coniunx una, meo praedita amans animo,
fido fida viro vixit studio parili, cum   5
  nulla in amaritie cessit ab officio.
     Aurelia Lucii liberta.

DESSAU, INSCRIPTIONES LATINAE SELECTAE NO. 7472

An Epitaph on Claudia

A husband praises his wife in this inscription from about 150 B.C. In the Greek manner, the inscription speaks to the passer-by, *hospes*, and asks him or her to stand near and read through the epitaph: *adsta ac perlege*.

hospes, itis, m, f stranger
deico = dico
paullum brief, slight, little
asto = adsto, are stand near
pellege = perlege: perlego, ere read through
heic = hic
sepulcrum, i, n tomb
hau = haud not, by no means
pulcrai = pulchrae
suom = suum
mareitum = maritum
cor, cordis, n heart
deilexit = dilexit: diligo, ere, dilexi love
souo = suo

5 *gnatos = natos: natus, i, m* son
creo, are bear, give birth to
horunc = horum of these (*i.e.*, sons)
linquo, ere leave behind
loco, are place
lepidus, a, um charming
tum autem and also
incessus, i, m manner
commodus, a, um pleasing
servo, are look after, keep
lana, ae, f wool: one of the main duties of the *matrona* was to oversee the making of the cloth for the household
abei = abi

An Epitaph on Aurelia

T his epitaph from Rome, c. 80 B.C., is inscribed on a statue of a man and a woman. The woman stands holding the man's right hand with both her own.

Lucii libertus the freedman of Lucius
lanius, i, m butcher
collis Viminalis Viminal Hill
praecedo, ere go ahead, yield beforehand
castus, a, um chaste
meo praedita animo possessed of my heart, mistress of my heart
5 *studium, i, n* keenness, enthusiasm
parilis, e similar, like, equal
nulla in amaritie = nulla in amaritia in no time of bitterness
cessit ab officio did she abandon her duty

PLINY MISSES HIS WIFE

C. PLINIUS CALPURNIAE SUAE S.

incredibile est quanto desiderio tui tenear. in causa
amor primum, deinde quod non consuevimus abesse.
inde est quod magnam noctium partem in imagine tua
vigil exigo; inde quod interdiu, quibus horis te visere 5
solebam, ad diaetam tuam ipsi me pedes ducunt; quod
denique aeger et maestus ac similis excluso a vacuo
limine recedo. unum tempus his tormentis caret, quo
in foro et amicorum litibus conteror. aestima tu, quae
vita mea sit, cui requies in labore, in miseria curisque 10
solacium. vale.

PLINY, *EPISTULAE VII.5*

CICERO WRITES TO HIS WIFE

TULLIUS S. D. TERENTIAE SUAE

in Tusculanum nos venturos putamus aut Nonis aut
postridie. ibi ut sint omnia parata. plures enim fortasse nobiscum erunt, et, ut arbitror, diutius ibi com-
morabimur. labrum si in balineo non est, ut sit. item 5
cetera, quae sunt ad victum et ad valetudinem
necessaria. vale.
  Kal. Oct. de Venusino

CICERO, *AD FAMILIARES XIV.20*

Pliny Misses His Wife

Pliny writes to his wife, Calpurnia, expressing his grief at their separation.

C. = Gaius
S. = *salutem dat* sends greetings
desiderium, i, n longing
teneo, ere hold
in causa amor primum the reason is first, love
consuesco, ere, evi am accustomed, am used to
inde est quod from this is the fact that; Tr. "this is why"
5 *vigil, ilis* awake
exigo, ere spend
interdiu in the daytime
viso, ere look at
diaeta, ae, f room

similis excluso Tr. "like a [lover] shut out"
vacuus, a, um empty
limen, inis, n threshold
recedo, ere go back, withdraw
tormentum, i, n torture, misery, torment
caret + abl. is free from
lis, litis, f lawsuit, legal controversy
contero, ere wear out
aestimo, are consider, judge
quae vita mea sit what my life is like
10 *cui requies (sit) in labore* for whom there is rest only in work
requies, etis, f rest, repose
solacium, i, n comfort, relief

Cicero Writes to His Wife

This is the last letter we have from Cicero to Terentia (47 B.C.). Curtness replaces the affectionate feelings of his earlier letters to his wife. The following year, Cicero and Terentia were divorced.

S.D. = *salutem dat* sends greetings
Tusculanum Tusculum: near Rome, the site of one of Cicero's villas
aut...aut either...or
Nonae October 7th
ibi ut sint omnia parata (fac) see to it that ...
diutius longer, quite a long time
commoror, ari stay, linger
5 *labrum, i, n* basin, tub

balineum, i, n bathroom
ut sit (fac) see to it that ...
item likewise
victus, us, m food
valetudo, inis, f good health, well-being
Kal. Oct. = Kalendae Octobres October 1st
Venusinum Venusia: site of one of Cicero's villas in the south of Italy

Martial Writes About Marriage

TWO WISE PEOPLE

nubere vis Prisco. non miror, Paula; sapisti.
    ducere te non vult Priscus. et ille sapit.

MARTIAL, *EPIGRAMS* IX.5

SEVEN DOWN

inscripsit tumulis septem scelerata virorum
    "se fecisse" Chloe. quid pote simplicius?

MARTIAL, *EPIGRAMS* IX.15

TIT FOR TAT

funera post septem nupsit tibi Galla virorum,
    Picentine. sequi vult, puto, Galla viros.

MARTIAL, *EPIGRAMS* IX.78

Two Wise People
METRE: ELEGIAC COUPLET

---

nubo, ere + dat. marry
sapio, ire, ii, be shrewd
duco, ere marry

Seven Down
METRE: ELEGIAC COUPLET

---

tumulus, i, m tomb
sceleratus, a, um wicked
*se fecisse = the usual formula used for
    erecting a memorial or tomb*
pote could be
simplicius more simple, franker

Tit for Tat
METRE: ELEGIAC COUPLET

---

funus, eris, n funeral
nubo, ere, nupsi + dat. marry
sequor, i follow
puto, are think

THE LEGACY HUNTER

petit Gemellus nuptias Maronillae
et cupit et instat et precatur et donat.
"adeone pulchra est?" immo, foedius nil est.
"quid ergo in illa petitur et placet?" tussit.

MARTIAL, *EPIGRAMS* I.10

MARITAL EQUALITY

uxorem quare locupletem ducere nolim
    quaeritis? uxori nubere nolo meae.
inferior matrona suo sit, Prisce, marito:
    non aliter fiunt femina virque pares.

MARTIAL, *EPIGRAMS* VIII.12

The Legacy Hunter
METRE: ELEGIAC COUPLET

---

peto, ere   seek
nuptiae, arum, f. pl.   marriage
insto, are   urge
precor, ari   beg
dono, are   give gifts
adeo   so
immo   no
foedior   uglier
ergo   therefore
tussio, ire   have a cough

Marital Equality
METRE: ELEGIAC COUPLET

---

quare   why
locuples, etis   rich
duco, ere   marry
nubo, ere + dat.   marry
maritus, i, m   husband
aliter   otherwise
par, is   equal

WIVES

Initial Questions

Pliny Writes About His Wife

1. Specify the features in Pliny's letter to his wife's aunt that read like an anecdotal report card.
2. Why does Pliny think he and his wife Calpurnia will continue to have a happy marriage?

Two Epitaphs on Wives

1. Which qualities of the wife does the epitaph on Claudia record? Do you think anything is missing from the description given in the epitaph?
2. In the epitaph on Aurelia, what wifely qualities does Lucius Hermia think are worth recording? What is the effect of the juxtaposition of *fido fida* in line 4?
3. Which epitaph gives a more vivid impression of the wife? Explain your answer.
4. Which husband reveals more affection?

Pliny Misses His Wife

1. What feelings for his wife does Pliny reveal in his letter to her? What three symptoms does he claim prove these feelings? Pick out the Latin words that show what Calpurnia contributes to their marriage.

Cicero Writes to His Wife

1. How would you feel on receiving a letter such as this one of Cicero to his wife? Specify the features in the letter that might be aggravating.

Martial Writes About Marriage

1. Coleridge, an English poet of the late eighteenth and early nineteenth century, defined an epigram in this way:
     "What is an Epigram? A dwarfish whole,
     Its body brevity, and wit its soul."
   For each of the Martial selections, consider how Martial uses brevity and wit to make his point.
2. By comparison with other writers in this section, what makes Martial's attitude to marriage distinctive? What is your attitude to the people in Martial's epigrams? How does your attitude compare with Martial's own attitude?

Discussion Questions

1. From Pliny's letter to his wife's aunt and from the two epitaphs, find any place (if such exist) where personal feelings of affection or love transcend the baldness of a catalogue of qualities.
2. Compare the tone of Pliny's letter to his wife with that of Cicero's letter to his wife.
3. What do you learn about the *husbands* in all these tributes and letters to wives?
4. Compare the different attitudes to wives and marriage the selections in this section reveal. Are any of these marriages of equals? Which seems to be the closest to your idea of a good marriage? Explain your answer.
5. Consider how the different audience and occasion for each of the selections in this section may, in part, account for the differences in tone.

Further Reading

A husband writes a poem to his dead wife: Ausonius, *Parentalia* IX.21-30.
Ovid illustrates the devotion and singleness of purpose of an old married couple, Baucis and Philemon: Ovid, *Metamorphoses* VIII.626ff.
Ovid relates the tragic story of Orpheus and Eurydice: Ovid, *Metamorphoses* X.1ff.
Pliny illustrates the devotion of Arria to her husband, Caecina Paetus, whom she follows in adversity even to the extent of sharing his suicide: Pliny, *Epistulae* III.16.

LOVERS

Wall painting of young girl with stylus and wax-covered writing tablet from Pompeii. (Naples, Naples National Museum)

An Echo of Sappho

ille mi par esse deo videtur,
ille, si fas est, superare divos,
qui sedens adversus identidem te
    spectat et audit
dulce ridentem, misero quod omnes   5
eripit sensus mihi; nam simul te,
Lesbia, aspexi, nihil est super mi
    vocis in ore;
lingua sed torpet, tenuis sub artus
flamma demanat, sonitu suopte   10
tintinant aures, gemina teguntur
    lumina nocte.

        CATULLUS, *CARMINA* 51

VIVAMUS, MEA LESBIA

vivamus, mea Lesbia, atque amemus,
rumoresque senum severiorum
omnes unius aestimemus assis!
soles occidere et redire possunt:
nobis cum semel occidit brevis lux,   5
nox est perpetua una dormienda.
da mi basia mille, deinde centum,
dein mille altera, dein secunda centum,
deinde usque altera mille, deinde centum,
dein, cum milia multa fecerimus,   10
conturbabimus illa, ne sciamus,
aut ne quis malus invidere possit,
cum tantum sciat esse basiorum.

        CATULLUS, *CARMINA* 5

An Echo of Sappho

METRE: SAPPHIC

Catullus vividly describes the intense sensations he experiences at the very sight of Lesbia with another man—perhaps her husband. The poem is a poetic imitation of an ode by Sappho, the renowned woman poet of love (c. 600 B.C.) from the Greek island of Lesbos.

mi = mihi
par equal
fas permitted, lawful; si fas est: if such is possible, if such is lawful
adversus, a, um opposite
identidem again and again
5 quod = id quod a situation that
eripio, ere + dat. (misero mihi) snatch away from
simul = simul atque as soon as
Lesbia pseudonym for Clodia, wife of Quintus Metellus Celer
aspicio, ere, aspexi catch sight of
est super = superest
nihil est super mi vocis in ore Tr. "there is no

sound left in my mouth"
lingua, ae, f tongue
torpeo, ere am numb
tenuis, e slender
artus, artus, m limbs, body
10 demano, are filter through
sonitu suopte with their own sound (-pte = an archaic emphatic suffix)
tintino, are ring, tinkle
geminus, a, um twin, both: metre proves this to be an ablative with nocte, but it is a transferred epithet belonging in meaning with lumina
tego, ere cover
lumina Tr. "eyes"

vivamus, mea Lesbia

METRE: HENDECASYLLABIC (PHALAECEAN)

This poem reflects an early stage in the progress of Catullus' love for Lesbia. Here Catullus expresses with passion and wit a universal theme of lovers: enjoy love now, since life is brief.

vivamus, amemus, aestimemus: pres. subjunctives let us ...
unius...assis Tr. "as worth a single coin": the as was a copper coin whose value, because of currency devaluations, decreased to the point where it was worth virtually nothing
5 occido, ere die, set
semel once
basia, n. pl. kisses
11 conturbabimus: a technical term in accounting.

The Romans, to erase a computation, had only to shake the abacus. The technical meaning of conturbare also includes intentionally falsifying statements of assets to shortchange creditors when declaring bankruptcy. Here Catullus says the lovers will confuse the tally of kisses intentionally to cheat the evil eye (invidere): Tr. "jumble the count"
invideo, ere Tr. "cast the evil eye"

TO LESBIA'S SPARROW

passer, deliciae meae puellae,
quicum ludere, quem in sinu tenere,
cui primum digitum dare adpetenti
et acres solet incitare morsus,
cum desiderio meo nitenti   5
carum nescio quid libet iocari,
et solaciolum sui doloris,
credo, tum gravis acquiescit ardor.
tecum ludere sicut ipsa possem
et tristes animi levare curas!   10

CATULLUS, CARMINA 2

ON THE DEATH OF LESBIA'S SPARROW

lugete, o Veneres Cupidinesque,
et quantum est hominum venustiorum.
passer mortuus est meae puellae,
passer, deliciae meae puellae.
quem plus illa oculis suis amabat: 5
nam mellitus erat suamque norat
ipsam tam bene quam puella matrem.
nec sese a gremio illius movebat,
sed circumsiliens modo huc modo illuc
ad solam dominam usque pipiabat.   10
qui nunc it per iter tenebricosum
illuc, unde negant redire quemquam.
at vobis male sit, malae tenebrae
Orci, quae omnia bella devoratis:
tam bellum mihi passerem abstulistis.   15
o factum male! o miselle passer!
tua nunc opera meae puellae
flendo turgiduli rubent ocelli.

CATULLUS, CARMINA 3

To Lesbia's Sparrow

METRE: HENDECASYLLABIC (PHALAECEAN)

Catullus' two poems to Lesbia's *passer* were among his most famous in ancient times. In this poem, Catullus envies the *passer* for the attentions lavished on it by Lesbia.

---

passer: Lesbia's *passer* is generally
  identified with the thrush or goldfinch
deliciae pet
quicum = cum quo
ludo, ere play
sinus, us, m lap, bosom
teneo, ere hold
primum digitum fingertip
adpetenti Tr. "for biting, pecking"
acer, acris sharp
morsus, us, m bite
5 *cum...libet* whenever it pleases
desiderium...nitens my shining sweetheart;

my light of desire
nitens, entis shining
carum iocari play an affectionate joke
nescio quid some...or other
solaciolum, i, n comfort, solace
dolor, oris, m torment of love
acquiesco, ere die down, be still
ardor, oris, m desire, passion
sicut just as
10 *tristis, e* sad
possem: pres. subj. would that I could
levo, are lighten
cura, ae, f care, passion

On the Death of Lesbia's Sparrow

METRE: HENDECASYLLABIC (PHALAECEAN)

This poem, ostensibly a lament on the death of Lesbia's *passer*, is a mock dirge. But the tone is affectionate and witty, not satiric, as Catullus turns the lament into a love poem.

---

lugeo, ere mourn, lament
o Veneres Cupidinesque all powers of Love
  and Desire
quantum...venustiorum Tr. "whatever rather
  tender-hearted men there be"
6 *mellitus, a, um* honey-sweet
suam = suam dominam
norat = noverat: nosco, ere, novi know
gremium, i, m lap
circumsilio, ire jump around
modo huc modo illuc now here, now there
10 *usque* constantly, continually
pipio, are chirp, cheep

tenebricosus, a, um shadowy, gloomy
vobis male sit woe to you, a curse on you
tenebrae, arum, f shades
Orcus, i, m Orcus, the god of the
  Underworld
15 *bellus, a, um* beautiful, lovely
aufero, ferre, abstuli steal away, take away
miselle: pathetic diminutive poor little
tua...opera: abl. by your doing
flendo from weeping
turgidulus, a, um swollen
rubeo, ere redden, am red
ocelli: pathetic diminutive poor little eyes

ETERNAL LOVE

iucundum, mea vita, mihi proponis amorem
   hunc nostrum inter nos perpetuumque fore.
di magni, facite ut vere promittere possit,
   atque id sincere dicat et ex animo,
ut liceat nobis tota perducere vita   5
   aeternum hoc sanctae foedus amicitiae.

               CATULLUS, *CARMINA* 109

ODI ET AMO

odi et amo. quare id faciam, fortasse requiris.
   nescio, sed fieri sentio et excrucior.

               CATULLUS, *CARMINA* 85

THE CONTRADICTORY BEHAVIOUR OF LESBIA

Lesbia mi dicit semper male nec tacet umquam
   de me: Lesbia me dispeream nisi amat.
quo signo? quia sunt totidem mea: deprecor illam
   assidue, verum dispeream nisi amo.

               CATULLUS, *CARMINA* 92

Eternal Love

METRE: ELEGIAC COUPLET

Catullus prays that Lesbia's view of their relationship may be like his: an everlasting bond.

---

iucundus, a, um pleasing
fore: fut. inf. of esse will be
facite ut grant that
vere truly
ex animo from the heart

5 *liceat nobis* we may be allowed
tota...vita: abl. in our entire lifetime
perduco, ere maintain, prolong
sanctus, a, um sacred, pure, holy
foedus, eris, n bond, treaty, contract

odi et amo

METRE: ELEGIAC COUPLET

Catullus poses a familiar paradox of love. The brevity of the statement only reinforces the dilemma.

---

quare why
requiro, ere ask
fieri happen
sentio, ire feel
excrucio, are torment

The Contradictory Behaviour of Lesbia

METRE: ELEGIAC COUPLET

Catullus continues his analysis of his love affair. In this poem, he attributes to Lesbia's behaviour the motives he finds in his own.

---

mi = mihi
taceo, ere be silent
dispeream ... nisi Tr. "may I be hanged if ...
  not..." or "let me be hanged if...not..."
quo signo by what sign? how do I know?

totidem just as many, equal
mea = mea verba
deprecor, ari cry out against
assidue constantly

FAITHLESSNESS

nulli se dicit mulier mea nubere malle
    quam mihi, non si se Iuppiter ipse petat.
dicit: sed mulier cupido quod dicit amanti,
    in vento et rapida scribere oportet aqua.

CATULLUS, CARMINA 70

TUA CULPA

huc est mens deducta tua mea, Lesbia, culpa
    atque ita se officio perdidit ipsa suo,
ut iam nec bene velle queat tibi, si optima fias,
    nec desistere amare, omnia si facias.

CATULLUS, CARMINA 75

Faithlessness

METRE: ELEGIAC COUPLET

A disillusioned Catullus analyzes the worth of a woman's word.

---

mulier, eris, f woman
nubo, ere + dat. marry
malo, malle prefer
peto, ere ask, seek
cupidus, a, um eager, passionate
amans, amantis, m lover
oportet ought

tua culpa

METRE: ELEGIAC COUPLET

Catullus again confesses his emotional dilemma, this time in an intimate exploration of love as physical fascination or respect.

---

huc here, to this point
deduco, ere, duxi, ductus lead, bring
tua...culpa: abl. by your fault, by your
   faithlessness
officio...suo: abl.
officium, i, n devotion
perdo, ere, perdidi destroy
ipsa = ipsa mens
bene velle + dat. to be fond of, to respect,
   to wish well
queat able to
fio, fieri become
desisto, ere cease, stop

MISER CATULLE

miser Catulle, desinas ineptire,
et quod vides perisse perditum ducas.
fulsere quondam candidi tibi soles,
cum ventitabas quo puella ducebat
amata nobis quantum amabitur nulla;   5
ibi illa multa cum iocosa fiebant
quae tu volebas nec puella nolebat;
fulsere vere candidi tibi soles.
nunc iam illa non vult: tu quoque impotens noli,
nec quae fugit sectare, nec miser vive,   10
sed obstinata mente perfer, obdura.
vale, puella. iam Catullus obdurat,
nec te requiret nec rogabit invitam.
at tu dolebis, cum rogaberis nulla.
scelesta, vae te, quae tibi manet vita?   15
quis nunc te adibit? cui videberis bella?
quem nunc amabis? cuius esse diceris?
quem basiabis? cui labella mordebis?
at tu, Catulle, destinatus obdura.

CATULLUS, CARMINA 8

miser Catulle

METRE: CHOLIAMBIC (SCAZONS)

Catullus, torn by disillusionment and love, remembers joys of the past, contemplates an empty future, and exhorts himself to break with Lesbia.

---

desinas ineptire Tr. "stop being a fool"
perisse = periisse: pereo, ire, ii, itus die, am lost
perditus, a, um lost
duco, ere consider, take, think
fulgeo, ere, fulsi shine
quondam once
candidus, a, um bright, dazzling
sol, is, m sun
ventito, are go
6 *iocosa, n. pl.* joys, fun
fio, fieri exist, happen, am
nec ... nolebat and ... did not refuse
impotens, entis powerless
10 *fugio, ere* flee, shun
sectare: imperative from secto, are follow
vivo, ere live
perfero, ferre endure
obduro, are harden one's heart
requiro, ere search for
doleo, ere be sorry
nulla not at all
15 *scelestus, a, um* wicked, wretched
vae te alas for you
videor, videri seem
bellus, a, um beautiful, lovely
cuius esse diceris? Whose will you be said to
    be? Tr. "Whose girl will they say you are?"
basio, are kiss
labellum, i, n lip
mordeo, ere bite, nibble
destinatus, a, um strong-minded, determined

PYRRHA

quis multa gracilis te puer in rosa
perfusus liquidis urget odoribus
    grato, Pyrrha, sub antro?
     cui flavam religas comam,
simplex munditiis? heu quotiens fidem 5
mutatosque deos flebit, et aspera
  nigris aequora ventis
    emirabitur insolens,
qui nunc te fruitur credulus aurea,
qui semper vacuam, semper amabilem 10
  sperat, nescius aurae
    fallacis! miseri, quibus
intemptata nites. me tabula sacer
votiva paries indicat uvida
  suspendisse potenti   15
    vestimenta maris deo.

> HORACE, *ODES* I.5

FINISHED WITH LOVE

vixi puellis nuper idoneus
et militavi non sine gloria;
  nunc arma defunctumque bello
    barbiton hic paries habebit,
laevum marinae qui Veneris latus   5
custodit. hic, hic ponite lucida
  funalia et vectis et arcus
    oppositis foribus minaces.
o quae beatam diva tenes Cyprum et
Memphim carentem Sithonia nive,   10
  regina, sublimi flagello
    tange Chloen semel arrogantem.

> HORACE, *ODES* III.26

Pyrrha

METRE: FOURTH ASCIEPIAD

From the vantage point of the escapee, Horace wonders what youth is entangled now in Pyrrha's love.

---

gracilis, e   slender

perfusus, a, um   drenched, bedewed

urgeo, ere   woo, court

gratus, a, um   pleasing

Pyrrha: the name, related to the Greek word for "fire", indicates that Pyrrha has the blond or auburn hair much admired by the Romans

antrum, i, n   cave

flavus, a, um   fair, blond

religo, are   tie, bind back

coma, ae, f   hair

5 munditia, ae, f   neatness, elegance

quotiens   how often

fidem = fidem mutatam

muto, are, avi, atus   change

fleo, ere   weep, bewail

asper, eris   dangerous, rough

niger, gra, grum   black, dark

emiror, ari   wonder at

insolens, entis   unfamiliar with, unaccustomed to

fruor, frui + abl.   enjoy

credulus, a, um   too believing, too trusting

aureus, a, um   golden (i.e., perfect)

10 vacuus, a, um   free, fancy-free

aura, ae, f   breeze

intemptatus, a, um   untried

niteo, ere   shine, am dazzling

tabula, ae, f   tablet, picture: sailors who had been saved from shipwreck often hung on the temple wall (sacer paries) a promised picture (tabula votiva) and their clothes (uvida vestimenta) to commemorate their gratitude for the rescue

tabula: abl.

votivus, a, um   promised by a vow

paries, ietis, f   wall

uvidus, a, um   dripping, wet

15 suspendo, ere   hang up

Finished With Love

METRE: ALCAIC

In this ode, Horace declares that he has withdrawn from the battles of love.

---

idoneus, a, um   pleasing

milito, are   serve as a soldier

barbitos, m, f: in acc. barbiton   lyre, lute

defungor, i, functus + abl.   finish, have done with

hic paries   this wall (i.e., of the temple of Venus)

5 laevum... latus   the left side (i.e., of the temple of Venus)

latus, eris, n   side, wall

marinus, a, um   of the sea, sea-born

lucidus, a, um   bright, blazing

funale, is, n   torch

vectis, is, m   crowbar, lever

arcus, us, m   bow

fores, um, f. pl.   doorway, gateway

minax, acis   full of menace

diva, ae, f   goddess (i.e., Venus)

teneo, ere   hold, rule over

Cyprus, i, f   Cyprus, an island in the Mediterranean sacred to Venus

10 Memphin: a Greek acc. Memphis, a city in Egypt where there was a famous temple to Venus

careo, ere + abl.   lack

Sithonius, a, um   Sithonian, Thracian: Thrace, now modern Bulgaria, is used to specify a country that gets snow

nix, nivis, f   snow

sublimis, e   lofty, uplifted

flagellum, i, m   whip, lash

THE QUARREL

"donec gratus eram tibi
nec quisquam potior bracchia candidae
    cervici iuvenis dabat,
Persarum vigui rege beatior."

"donec non alia magis   5
arsisti neque erat Lydia post Chloen,
    multi Lydia nominis
Romana vigui clarior Ilia."

"me nunc Thressa Chloe regit,
dulces docta modos et citharae sciens,   10
    pro qua non metuam mori,
si parcent animae fata superstiti."

"me torret face mutua
Thurini Calais filius Ornyti,
    pro quo bis patiar mori,   15
si parcent puero fata superstiti."

"quid si prisca redit Venus
diductosque iugo cogit aeneo,
    si flava excutitur Chloe
reiectaeque patet ianua Lydiae?"   20

"quamquam sidere pulchrior
ille est, tu levior cortice et improbo
    iracundior Hadria,
tecum vivere amem, tecum obeam libens."

HORACE, *ODES* III.9

The Quarrel

METRE: SECOND ASCLEPIAD

This poem is the only one that Horace wrote in dialogue form. The lovers' quarrel and reconciliation is a verbal contest between Lydia and her lover (perhaps Horace himself) in which the lady caps each argument of her lover.

---

donec as long as
gratus, a, um pleasing, acceptable
nec quisquam potior iuvenis and no other more favoured young man
bracchium, i, n arm
candidus, a, um shining, fair
cervix, icis, f neck
dabat = circumdabat bracchia + dat. put his arms around
Persarum rege: abl. of comparison than the King of Persia: the King of Persia was proverbially rich and happy
vigeo, ere, vigui flourish, live
beatior, ius happier
5 *alia: abl.* because of some other girl
magis more
ardeo, ere, arsi burn with love
post + acc. behind, second to
multi nominis of great renown
Romana Ilia: abl. of comparison than Roman Ilia: Ilia was the mother of Romulus and Remus
rego, ere rule
10 *modi, orum, m* musical strains, measures
cithara, ae, f lyre, lute
sciens, entis + gen. skilled, expert
metuo, ere fear
morior, mori die
parco, ere + dat. spare
anima, ae, f darling
superstes, stitis surviving, living
torreo, ere burn, consume

fax, facis, f torch, flame of love
Thurini of Thurii: a Greek colony in southern Italy, with a reputation for luxury and wealth
15 *bis* twice
patior, pati endure
priscus, a, um old, ancient, early
Venus Love: Venus, goddess and symbol of love
diductus, a, um separated, divided
iugum, i, n yoke
cogo, ere unite, bring together
aeneus, a, um bronze
flavus, a, um fair-haired, golden-haired
excutio, ere shake off
20 *reicio, ere, ieci, iectus* reject
pateo, ere be open
quamquam although
sidere: abl. of comparison than a star
sidus, eris, n star
levis, e light
cortice: abl. of comparison than a cork
cortex, corticis, m cork
improbus, a, um restless, unstable
iracundus, a, um passionate, angry
Hadria: abl. of comparison than the Adriatic
Hadria, ae, m Adriatic Sea, notorious for sudden storms
amem, obeam: present subjunctives
amo, are love
obeo, ire die, perish
libens, libentis willingly, gladly

CHLOE

vitas inuleo me similis, Chloe,
quaerenti pavidam montibus aviis
  matrem non sine vano
    aurarum et siluae metu.
nam seu mobilibus veris inhorruit   5
adventus foliis seu virides rubum
  dimovere lacertae,
    et corde et genibus tremit.
atqui non ego te tigris ut aspera
Gaetulusve leo frangere persequor: 10
  tandem desine matrem
    tempestiva sequi viro.

HORACE, ODES I.23

A PARADOX

difficilis facilis, iucundus acerbus es idem:
  nec tecum possum vivere nec sine te.

MARTIAL, EPIGRAMS XII.47

Chloe

METRE: FOURTH ASCLEPIAD

H orace exhorts timid Chloe to stop fleeing from love.

---

vito, are avoid, flee from
inuleus, i, m fawn
similis, e + dat. like, similar to
Chloe: from a Greek word meaning "fresh, green, young"
quaero, ere seek
pavidus, a, um timid, frightened
avius, a, um out of the way, trackless
non sine vano...metu in needless fear
aura, aurae, f wind, breath of air
siluae = silvae; silva, ae, f wood, forest
5 *seu...seu* whether...or
mobilis, e quivering
ver, veris, n spring
inhorresco, ere, horrui rustle, shiver
adventus, us, m approach
folium, i, n leaf

viridis, e green
rubus, i, m bramble, briar
dimovere = dimoverunt move
lacerta, ae, f lizard
cor, cordis, n heart
genu, genus, n knee
tigris, is, m or f tiger
ut as
asper, aspera, asperum fierce
10 *Gaetulus, a, um* Getulian, a north African tribe
frangere: inf. after persequor to indicate purpose to maul
persequor, sequi pursue, follow
desino, ere stop
tempestivus, a, um of an age for
vir, viri, m husband

A Paradox

METRE: ELEGIAC COUPLET

M artial offers yet another version of the age-old problem of love.

---

iucundus, a, um pleasant
acerbus, a, um sour, bitter
idem in the same person

LOVERS

Initial Questions

An Echo of Sappho
1. There has been much scholarly agonizing over whether this is the first poem in the cycle that explores the turbulent relationship between Catullus and Lesbia. In any case, it is clear that the poem is meant to portray an early stage in the affair. What are Catullus' emotional and physical reactions on seeing Lesbia with another man?

vivamus, mea Lesbia
1. (a) What is an Epicurean argument?
    (b) What Epicurean argument does Catullus use in this poem? How persuasive is this argument in the context of Catullus' proposition? Consider also, in this connection, the tone of the poem.
2. Find all the images that relate (a) to unity or singleness and (b) to multiplicity in *vivamus, mea Lesbia*. How do these images contribute to the theme of the poem?

To Lesbia's Sparrow
1. Carefully outline the structural shifts from bird to girl to poet. Using this reconstruction as a starting point, explore the subsurface of the poem in terms of the symbolism of the bird in its relationship (a) to Lesbia and (b) to Catullus himself.

On the Death of Lesbia's Sparrow
1. This poem purports to be a dirge, that is, a song or hymn expressing deep grief and a solemn sense of loss.
    (a) Consider what devices in the poem (*e.g.*, sound effects, repetition, etc.) are suitable for a poem about death.
    (b) What devices does Catullus use to alter the tone and change a lament into a love poem?

Eternal Love
1. Catullus here gives us his definition of *amor*. What exactly does Catullus want from his relationship with Lesbia? Pay close attention to the shift of addressees and the specific words Catullus carefully chooses to connote a relationship beyond the physical.

odi et amo
1. "*ars est celare artem*" might have been written with Catullus' *odi et amo* in mind. Examine word order, diction (especially the verbs), and structure. Show what each contributes to the impact of the theme.

The Contradictory Behaviour of Lesbia
1. Study the parallel structure in this poem. What significance has the parallelism to the theme of the poem?

Faithlessness
1. Consider how Catullus uses repetition, parallelism, emphatic word order, diction, exaggeration, and imagery all to reflect his tone of bitterness and disillusionment.

tua culpa
1. The use of the couplet is particularly suited to paradoxical statement. Examine the balanced structure and antitheses of *tua culpa* and show what they suggest about the Catullus-Lesbia relationship.

miser Catulle
1. *miser Catulle* seems most modern in its use of the interior monologue popular in twentieth-century poetry. Carefully analyze the structure of the poem and show how it has been artistically calculated to reflect Catullus' confusion.

Pyrrha
1. Show how Horace here uses a series of contrasts and visual word pictures to create and sustain tone.
2. Examine this poem carefully to see where and how Horace uses sea metaphors. What does this imagery contribute to our understanding (a) of Pyrrha and (b) of Horace's attitude to love?

Finished With Love
1. Study closely the sustained imagery in this poem. What is Horace saying about love by using such images? What are the indications of Horace's attitude: is he an amused onlooker or a participant?

The Quarrel
1. Carefully examine word echoes, parallelism, and balanced antithesis. What is the significance of such deliberate structural organization for the revelation of the theme?

Chloe
1. Show how Horace uses the introductory image of Chloe as a timid deer (a) to unify his poem and (b) to reveal both Chloe's attitude and Horace's attitude to love.

A Paradox
1. How does Martial use diction to reveal the bittersweet relationship of lovers in this couplet?

Discussion Questions
1. Re-examine Catullus' poems in this section and analyze the extent to which his language of love reflects the changes in his attitude to Lesbia.
2. Compare Catullus and Horace as poets: consider the treatment by each of a similar theme, the attitude of each to his situation, and the intention of each in writing love poetry.
3. Many of the poems in this section have inspired poetic imitations in English. Analyze some poetic imitations of a particular poem and write a critical appreciation in which you evaluate the extent to which each imitator has used diction, rhythm, imagery, emphatic techniques, etc., to capture the spirit of the original. For Catullus' *vivamus, mea Lesbia*, you might examine imitations by Thomas Campion, Ben Jonson, and Frank Copley. For Horace's *Pyrrha*, you might collect imitations by John Milton, Gilbert Highet, Franklin Adams, and Eugene Field.

4. There are other lovers' poems of rivalry in dialogue form besides Horace's "The Quarrel" (*e.g.*, "Acme and Septimius" by Catullus (*Carmina* 45), and "Willy and Philly" by Robert Burns). Compare two or more of these poems, considering such poetic aspects as tone, sound, imagery, and organization.

Further Reading

Catullus writes that no woman has been loved as much as Lesbia was loved by him: Catullus, *Carmina* 87.

Catullus writes that Lesbia's unfaithfulness has destroyed the unique kind of love he had for her: Catullus, *Carmina* 72.

Catullus tells Lesbia how many kisses will satisfy him: Catullus, *Carmina* 7.

Horace admonishes Lydia for ruining Sybaris with her love: Horace, *Odes* I.8.

Horace writes that he will always love his Lalage: Horace, *Odes* I.22.

Ovid takes a girl to the races: Ovid, *Amores* III.ii, 1ff.

Pygmalion creates the perfect woman: Ovid, *Metamorphoses* X. 243-297.

Ovid records the tragic love story of Pyramus and Thisbe: Ovid, *Metamorphoses* IV.55ff.

Vergil tells the famous love story of Aeneas and Dido: Vergil, *Aeneid* IV.

FAMILY

Family tombstone of Lucius Vibius, his wife, and their son. (Rome, Vatican Museum)

TULLIA'S ILLNESS

TULLIUS TERENTIAE SUAE S. D.

in maximis meis doloribus excruciat me valetudo
Tulliae nostrae. de qua nihil est, quod ad te plura
scribam: tibi enim aeque magnae curae esse certe scio.
quod me propius vultis accedere, video ita esse facien- 5
dum. etiam ante fecissem, sed me multa impediverunt,
quae ne nunc quidem expedita sunt. sed a Pomponio
exspecto litteras, quas ad me quam primum perferendas cures velim. da operam ut valeas.

CICERO, *AD FAMILIARES* XIV.19

Tullia's Illness

Cicero writes his wife expressing his anxiety over their daughter's illness.

S.D. = *salutem dat* sends greetings

maximis meis doloribus: Cicero has just
  returned from Greece after Caesar's
  decisive defeat of Pompey in the
  summer of 48 B.C. at the battle of
  Pharsalus in northeast Greece. This
  battle ended the First Triumvirate.
  After much agonizing, Cicero had
  joined Pompey's side in the conflict.

dolor, oris, m grief, sorrow

excrucio, are torment, distress

valetudo, inis, f health, state of health; here
  "ill-health"

plura more, further

cura, ae, f worry, anxiety

5 *quod...vultis + acc. and inf.* as to your wish
  that...

propius closer, nearer: Terentia was in Rome,
  Cicero at Brundisium, the harbour on
  the southeast coast of Italy from which
  the Romans made the crossing to
  countries east of Italy

accedo, ere come (to)

impedio, ire hinder, impede

expedio, ire, ivi, itus set right, disentangle

Pomponius: Titus Pomponius Atticus was
  Cicero's closest friend

*quas ad me quam primum perferendas cures
  velim* I would like you to see that they
  are delivered to me as soon as possible

da operam see to it (that), take care (to)

Interested In-Laws

I. CICERO ATTICO SAL.

ad me scribis de sorore tua; ipsa testis erit tibi quan-
tae mihi curae fuerit ut animus Quinti fratris in eam
esset is, qui esse deberet. cum eum esse offensiorem
arbitrarer, eas litteras ad eum misi quibus et placarem 5
ut fratrem et monerem ut minorem et obiurgarem ut
errantem. confido ita esse omnia ut velimus.

CICERO, *AD ATTICUM* I.5

II. CICERO ATTICO SAL.

vidi nihil tam mite, nihil tam placatum, quam tum
meus frater erat in sororem tuam. si fuerat ex ratione
sumptus offensio, non appareret.

postridie Arpino profecti sumus et prandimus in Ar- 5
cano. humanissime Quintus "Pomponia," inquit, "tu
invita mulieres, ego ascivero viros." nihil potuit dulcius
verbis et animo et vultu. at illa, audientibus nobis, "ego
ipsa sum," inquit, "hic hospita." id ex eo, ut opinor,
quod Statius antecesserat, ut prandium nobis videret. 10
tum Quintus "en," inquit mihi, "haec ego patior
cotidie." me ipsum commoverat: sic absurde et aspere
verbis vultuque responderat. dissimulavi dolens.
discubuimus omnes praeter illam. cui tamen Quintus
de mensa misit. illa reiecit. quid multa? nihil meo fratre 15
lenius, nihil asperius tua sorore mihi visum est.

CICERO, *AD ATTICUM* V.1

Interested In-laws

I. In this excerpt from a letter to his good friend Atticus, Cicero hopes he has successfully ended the quarrelling of Pomponia, Atticus' sister, and her husband Quintus, Cicero's brother. At Atticus' request, Cicero has talked with his brother about treating his wife better.

Sal. = *salutem dat* sends greetings
testis, is, m or f witness
animus, i, m the disposition, the feeling
is qui esse deberet what it ought to be
offensus, a, um displeasing
5 *arbitror, ari* judge, perceive
placo, are calm
minor, oris junior, younger
obiurgo, are scold
errans, antis one in the wrong
confido, ere trust

II. Sixteen years later, Pomponia and Quintus are still quarrelling, and Cicero and Atticus are still involving themselves in the family problems. In this letter, Cicero reports to Atticus on a visit to his brother and his brother's wife.

Sal. = *salutem dat* sends greetings
tam...quam as...as
mitis, e gentle
placatus, a, um quiet, gentle, calm
ex ratione sumptus offensio a quarrel about expenses
5 *Arpinum, i, n* Arpinum: Cicero's birthplace, a town southeast of Rome
prando, ere eat lunch
Arcanum, i, n Arcanum: a villa owned by Quintus south of Arpinum
humane kindly
ascisco, ere, ascivi receive, welcome
potuit = *potuit esse*
dulcius: comparative adv. sweeter
verbis, animo, vultu: ablatives of comparison than his words, his disposition, his face
illa marks a change of speaker (i.e., Pomponia)
hospita, ae guest

id ex eo quod this (outburst) was from the fact that
10 *Statius:* one of Quintus' slaves
antecedo, ere, cessi go in front, go before
videret = *provideret* see to, provide
commoveo, ere, movi upset, disturb
aspere harshly
dissimulo, are, avi hide feelings
dolens although I was grieving
discumbo, ere, cubui recline at table
praeter + acc. except
15 *de mensa misit* sent (food) from the table
reicio, ere, ieci reject
quid multa? why say more?, what more should I say?
meo fratre...tua sorore: ablatives of comparison than my brother...than your sister
lenius: comparative from lenis, e kind
pluribus = *pluribus verbis*
instituo, ere instruct

39

A Letter of Condolence

SER. SULPICIUS S. D. M. T. CICERONI

postquam mihi nuntiatum est de obitu Tulliae, filiae
tuae, graviter tuli, communemque eam calamitatem
existimavi. genus hoc consolationis miserum atque
acerbum est. tamen decrevi brevi ad te scribere.   5
   quae res mihi consolationem tulit, volo tibi
commemorare—si forte eadem res tibi dolorem
minuere possit. ex Asia rediens, coepi regiones circumcirca prospicere. post me erat Aegina, ante me Megara,
dextra Piraeus, sinistra Corinthus. quae oppida quon- 10
dam tempore florentissima fuerunt; nunc prostrata iacent. coepi egomet mecum sic cogitare: "hem! nos
homunculi indignamur, si quis nostrum interiit, cum
uno loco tot oppidorum cadavera proiecta iacent?" si
illa hoc tempore non periisset, paucis post annis tamen 15
ei moriendum fuit, quoniam homo nata fuerat.
   cogita, quemadmodum adhuc fortuna nobiscum
egerit. ea nobis erepta esse, quae non minus quam
liberi, cara esse debent—patriam, honestatem,
dignitatem, honores omnes. quid hoc unum incom- 20
modum ad dolorem adiungere potuit? nuper uno tempore tot viri clarissimi interierunt; imperium populi
Romani labefactum est; omnes provinciae con-
quassatae sunt. mors unius mulierculae te commovet?
   reminiscere: illam te, patrem suum, praetorem, con- 25
sulem, augurem vidisse; cum res publica occideret, vita
excessisse. quid est quod tu aut illa cum fortuna queri
possitis? noli te oblivisci Ciceronem esse.

CICERO, *AD FAMILIARES* IV.5

A Letter of Condolence

In 45 B.C., Cicero's beloved daughter Tullia died after giving birth to a son. In this famous letter of condolence, one of Cicero's close friends, Servius Sulpicius Rufus, writes in hope of easing Cicero's grief.

Ser. = Servius
S.D. = salutem dat sends greetings
M. = Marcus
T. = Tullius
obitus, us, m death
communis, e shared, general, universal
existimo, are, avi consider, think
genus, eris, n kind, type
5 acerbus, a, um bitter
decerno, ere, crevi decide
commemoro, are relate
forte perhaps
dolor, oris, m grief, anguish, pain
minuo, uere make smaller, diminish
coepi I began
circumcirca all round about
prospicio, ere look at
10 quondam tempore at one time
florens, entis flourishing, prosperous
prostratus, a, um ruined, laid low
iaceo, ere lie
egomet: -met is an emphatic suffix
hem alas
homunculi: pathetic diminutive poor mortals
indignor, ari complain
intereo, ire, ii die
cadaver, eris, n dead, corpse; metaphorically,
  ruins of towns
proiectus, a, um stretched out
15 illa indicates change in subject (i.e., Tullia)
morior, mori die
quoniam since

homo, inis mortal, human
natus, a, um born
cogito, are consider
quemadmodum how
adhuc up to now
ago, ere, egi deal
nobis from us
eripio, ere, ui, reptus snatch away, tear away
ea nobis erepta...honores omnes: Sulpicius is
  referring to the recent civil wars between
  Pompey and Caesar, during which Pompey,
  the man he and Cicero had supported, was
  defeated by Caesar
carus, a, um dear, precious
patria, ae, f homeland
20 incommodum, i, n inconvenience, misfortune
adiungo, ere add
nuper recently
imperium, i, n rule, authority, power:
  Sulpicius means that Rome has lost prestige
  from the civil wars
labefacio, ere, feci, factus weaken, under-
  mine, overthrow
conquasso, are, avi, atus shatter, shake
muliercula: pathetic diminutive little woman
25 reminiscere: imperative from reminiscor, i
  remember
res publica, rei publicae, f state, republic
occido, ere die
vita excedo, ere, cessi die
queror, i complain (of)
obliviscor, i forget

THE REPLY

M. T. C. S. D. SER. SULPICIO

ego vero, Servi, vellem, ut scribis, in meo gravissimo
casu adfuisses. litteris lectis, aliquantum acquievi. nam
et ea scripsisti quae levare luctum possent et in me con-
solando non mediocrem ipse dolorem adhibuisti. turpe 5
esse existimo, me non ferre casum meum, ut tu, tali
sapientia praeditus, ferendum putas. sed opprimor interdum et vix resisto dolori. mihi, amissis ornamentis
eis, quae ipse commemoras, unum illud solacium
manebat. habebam filiam ad quam confugerem, ubi 10
conquiescerem, cuius in sermone omnes curas dolores-
que deponerem. nunc autem a republica maestus
fugere non possum. itaque et domo absum et foro,
quod nec domus eum dolorem, quem de republica
capio, consolari potest, nec domesticum respublica. 15
  quo magis te exspecto teque videre quam primum
cupio.

CICERO, *AD FAMILIARES* IV.6

The Reply

Cicero writes an answer to Sulpicius in which he reveals the close relationship he had enjoyed with his daughter.

M.T.C. = *Marcus Tullius Cicero*
S.D. = *salutem dat* sends greetings
Ser. = *Servio*
vero indeed, truly
gravis, e serious, grievous
casus, us, m calamity, mischance
lego, ere, legi, lectus read
aliquantum some little
acquiesco, ere, quievi find comfort
levo, are lighten
luctus, us, m grief
5 *non mediocrem* not inconsiderable
dolor, oris, m pain
adhibeo, ere, ui bring to bear
turpe: n. sg. disgraceful
existimo, are think
ut as, in the way that
talis, e such
praeditus, a, um + abl. endowed with, possessing
puto, are consider, think
opprimo, ere overcome, press down

interdum sometimes
vix hardly, scarcely
resisto, ere + dat. resist
amitto, ere, misi, missus lose
ornamentum, i, n honour, distinction
commemoro, are mention
solacium, i, n solace, comfort
10 *confugerem, conquiescerem, deponerem: imperf. subjunctives in rel. clauses of purpose* I might flee for refuge, might find rest, might put aside
confugio, ere + ad flee for refuge to
conquiesco, ere find rest
depono, ere put aside
foro (i.e., public business, probably at the law courts which were situated in the Basilica Iulia in the Roman Forum)
15 *consolor, ari* comfort, ease
domesticus, a, um domestic, family
quo magis therefore all the more
quam primum as soon as possible

A Brother's Death

multas per gentes et multa per aequora vectus
    advenio has miseras, frater, ad inferias,
ut te postremo donarem munere mortis
    et mutam nequiquam alloquerer cinerem.
quandoquidem fortuna mihi tete abstulit ipsum,   5
    heu miser indigne frater adempte mihi,
nunc tamen interea haec prisco quae more parentum
    tradita sunt tristi munere ad inferias,
accipe fraterno multum manantia fletu,
    atque in perpetuum, frater, ave atque vale.   10

CATULLUS, *CARMINA* 101

Tombstone for a Daughter

D. M. S.

Calliste vixit annis XVI mes III hor VI et s;
nuptura idibus Oct, moritur III idus Octobres;
Panathenais mater pia car fil fecit.

BARROW, *LATIN INSCRIPTIONS* No. 144

A Brother's Death

METRE: ELEGIAC COUPLET

Catullus' brother died at an early age in Asia Minor, not far from the site of ancient Troy. In 57 B.C., on his way to Bithynia, a Roman province situated where modern Turkey is today, Catullus visited his brother's tomb to make the traditional offerings. To mark the occasion of his mournful visit, Catullus wrote this eloquent elegy expressing his grief.

---

aequor, oris, n sea

vectus, a, um carried: from *veho*

inferiae, arum, f. pl. funeral sacrifices, funeral offerings: such offerings would include wine, milk, honey, flowers, and perhaps this poem

munus, eris, n gift, tribute

nequiquam in vain, vainly (Compare *mutam:* Catullus will receive no answer.)

alloquor, i address, speak to

5 *quandoquidem* since

mihi: from me

tete: -te is an emphatic suffix

aufero, ferre, abstuli steal, take away

heu...mihi: an interjection

indigne undeservedly, cruelly

adempte stolen, taken away

priscus, a, um old, early

mos, moris, m custom

haec: obj. of accipe, line 9 these tokens, these gifts

tristi munere as a sad gift, as a tribute of grief

manantia: modifies haec

manans, tis wet, drenched

fletus, us, m weeping, tears

10 *ave atque vale* hail and farewell: traditional formula of farewell to the dead

---

Tombstone for a Daughter

This inscription was found on a tombstone in Tipasa, a Roman town in northwest Africa.

D(is) M(anibus) S(acrum) sacred to the spirit of the dead

mes = mensibus

s = semisse a half

nuptura: fut. part. about to wed

idibus Oct October 15th

morior, i die

pius, a, um devoted, affectionate

car = carae dear, precious

fil = filiae

FAMILY

Initial Questions

Tullia's Illness

1. What does Cicero reveal about his feelings for (a) his wife and (b) his daughter? How does he reveal these feelings?
2. Compare Cicero's attitude to Terentia in this letter of 48 B.C. with that shown in his letter of 47 B.C. on page 6.

Interested In-laws

1. Compare (a) the tone of these two letters and (b) Cicero's changing attitude towards Quintus and Pomponia concerning their responsibility for their marital difficulties.

A Letter of Condolence

1. Analyze carefully the arguments used by Servius Sulpicius to console a father on the death of a daughter. How persuasive do you find each of these consolations?

The Reply

1. How persuasive does Cicero seem to find each of Servius Sulpicius' arguments? How does this letter reveal Cicero's love for his daughter?

A Brother's Death

1. Here Catullus changes a conventional form used on tombstones into a personal lament. Write a critical appreciation of the poem in which you consider how all elements of the poem create and sustain the pathos. You should examine, among other things, the poet's use of sound, alliteration, repetition, interjection, word order, and the contrast between ritual observance and personal observance.

Tombstone for a Daughter

1. Find the only two words that express emotion in this epitaph. What is the effect of each of these words? Does any other detail in the epitaph prepare you for the use of either of these adjectives? What would be the difference in the tone of the epitaph if either or both of these adjectives had been omitted?

Discussion Questions

1. Referring to specific poems read in this section, compare Roman and modern attitudes towards family difficulties such as illness, death, and marital quarrelling.
2. Compare Cicero's "The Reply," Catullus' "A Brother's Death," and "A Tombstone for a Daughter." What is the purpose of each writer? How effective is each writer in achieving his purpose? Which writer do you find the most moving? Which the least moving? Why?

Further Reading

From exile in the east, Cicero writes his wife, daughter, and son: Cicero, *ad Familiares* XIV.2. Horace writes a tribute to his father in a moving portrait of a man who, although a freedman, acted as Horace's *paedagogus* when Horace was getting his education: Horace, *Satires* I.vi, 71-89.

FRIENDS

Part of the sarcophagus of Lucius Aemilius Daphnus: boys playing with nuts. Sc. 2321, A. H. Smith, *A Catalogue of Sculpture in the Department of Greek and Roman Antiquities, British Museum*, Vols. I-III (1896-1904) (London, British Museum)

ON THE DEATH OF MARTIAL

C. PLINIUS CORNELIO PRISCO SUO S.

audio Valerium Martialem decessisse et moleste fero.
erat homo ingeniosus, acutus, acer, et qui plurimum
in scribendo et salis habebat et fellis, nec minus can-
doris. prosecutus eram viatico in Hispaniam 5
secedentem: dederam hoc amicitiae, dederam etiam
versiculis, quos de me composuit.

   meritone eum nunc ut amicissimum defunctum esse
doleo? dedit enim mihi quantum maximum potuit,
daturus amplius si potuisset. tametsi quid homini 10
potest dari maius, quam gloria et laus et aeternitas?
at non erunt aeterna quae scripsit: non erunt fortasse,
ille tamen scripsit tamquam essent futura. vale.

PLINY, EPISTULAE III.21

On the Death of Martial

Pliny is saddened by news of the death of his friend Martial. The date of Martial's death is unknown. Martial retired c. A.D. 98 to his native town Bilbilis in Spain. From there, he wrote his last book of epigrams in A.D. 101.

C. = Gaius
S. = *salutem dat* sends greetings
decedo, ere, decessi die
moleste fero, ferre find hard to bear
ingeniosus, a, um talented
acutus, a, um sharp, keen, intelligent
acer, cris, cre shrewd, sharp, cutting
plurimum much
sal, salis, m salt, wit
fel, fellis, n gall, bitterness
minus + gen. less
candor, oris, m frankness, fairness
prosecutus eram I had seen him off
viaticum, i, n travelling expenses
secedens, entis retiring
versiculus, i, m little verse
merito it is right, worthy
amicissimus, a, um Tr. "very dear friend"
defungor, i, functus die
doleo, ere grieve, mourn
quantum maximum as much as
amplius more
tametsi although
maius more
laus, laudis, m praise
aeternitas, atis, f immortality
at...scripsit: an imagined objection from the
  receiver of the letter, Cornelius Priscus
fortasse perhaps
tamquam as if

49

To Fabullus

cenabis bene, mi Fabulle, apud me
paucis, si tibi di favent, diebus,
si tecum attuleris bonam atque magnam
cenam, non sine candida puella
et vino et sale et omnibus cachinnis.   5
haec si, inquam, attuleris, venuste noster,
cenabis bene: nam tui Catulli
plenus sacculus est aranearum.
sed contra accipies meros amores
seu quid suavius elegantiusve est: 10
nam unguentum dabo, quod meae puellae
donarunt Veneres Cupidinesque,
quod tu cum olfacies, deos rogabis,
totum ut te faciant, Fabulle, nasum.

CATULLUS, *CARMINA* 13

To Cicero

disertissime Romuli nepotum,
quot sunt quotque fuere, Marce Tulli,
quotque post aliis erunt in annis,
gratias tibi maximas Catullus
agit pessimus omnium poeta,   5
tanto pessimus omnium poeta,
quanto tu optimus omnium es patronus.

CATULLUS, *CARMINA* 49

To Fabullus

METRE: HENDECASYLLABIC (PHALAECEAN)

Catullus invites his friend Fabullus to dinner. But the invitation holds an unusual twist.

---

mi Fabulle Fabullus was a close friend of Catullus

tibi: humorously substituted for the *mihi* usual in formulas of this kind

di = dei

non sine together with, not forgetting

candidus, a, um shining

sal, salis, m salt, wit

omnibus cachinnis all kinds of laughter

venustus, a, um charming, gracious, dear: to be *venustus* was an attribute most valued by those belonging to Catullus' circle of friends

sacculus, i, m: pathetic diminutive poor little purse

plenus aranearum full of cobwebs

aranea, ae, f cobweb

contra in return

meros amores pure affection, real love: *merum* was pure, unwatered wine

10 *seu quid suavius elegantiusve est* or if there is anything sweeter or more exquisite; or whatever there is

unguentum, i, n perfume: usually provided by the host at any expensive Roman banquet

meae puellae: dat.

donarunt = donaverunt

dono, are, avi give, present

Veneres Cupidinesque: poetic plural: together Venus, goddess of love and beauty, and Cupid, her son, represented all the powers of love.

olfacio, ere smell

nasus, i, m nose

To Cicero

METRE: HENDECASYLLABIC (PHALAECEAN)

This poem is addressed to the famous orator Marcus Tullius Cicero. The circumstances that inspired the poem are unknown—although there has been much scholarly speculation! For instance, it has been speculated that Cicero helped Catullus in a lawsuit. Another suggestion is that Catullus is thanking Cicero for providing his house as a meeting place for Catullus and Lesbia.

---

disertus, a, um eloquent

Romuli nepos, otis descendant of Romulus

Marce Tulli: the formal style of address, alluding to Cicero's public importance, especially in the Senate

post hereafter

tanto...quanto as much...as

patronus, i, m lawyer, advocate

To Veranius

Verani, omnibus e meis amicis
antistans mihi milibus trecentis,
venistine domum ad tuos Penates
fratresque unanimos anumque matrem?
venisti. o mihi nuntii beati!   5
visam te incolumem audiamque Hiberum
narrantem loca, facta, nationes,
ut mos est tuus, applicansque collum
iucundum os oculosque suaviabor.
o quantum est hominum beatiorum,   10
quid me laetius est beatiusve?

            CATULLUS, *CARMINA* 9

To Cornificius

male est, Cornifici, tuo Catullo,
male est, me hercule, et laboriose,
et magis magis in dies et horas.
quem tu, quod minimum facillimumque est,
qua solatus es allocutione?   5
irascor tibi. sic meos amores?
paulum quid libet allocutionis,
maestius lacrimis Simonideis.

            CATULLUS, *CARMINA* 38

To Veranius

METRE: HENDECASYLLABIC (PHALAECEAN)

Catullus expresses delight at the news that his friend Veranius has returned home from Spain where Veranius and Fabullus had been on the governor's staff.

---

antistans + dat. worth as much (to me) as...
Penates household gods: symbol of the home and the family
unanimus, a, um affectionate, of one mind
anus, anus, f old woman; *as an adjective:* aged
5 *nuntius, i, m* news
incolumis, e safe, unharmed
Hiberum gen. pl. of the Spaniards
mos, oris m custom, habit
applicans drawing towards me

collum: obj. of applicans
collum, i, n, neck
iucundus, a, um sweet, charming
os, oris, n mouth
suavior, ari kiss
10 *quantum est hominum beatiorum* as much as there is of quite happy men; Tr. "whatever happy men there be"
me: abl. of comparison than me
-ve or

To Cornificius

METRE: HENDECASYLLABIC (PHALAECEAN)

Quintus Cornificius was a poet and friend of Catullus. He, like Catullus, was a member of the *poetae neoteroi*. Here, Catullus, feeling particularly depressed, rebukes his friend for neglecting him. The occasion for the poem is not known, though some suggest that Catullus has received word of his brother's death.

---

male est things are bad
Cornifici: voc.
laboriose painfully so
quem him (i.e., Catullus)
quod...est: an interjection
5 *qua allocutione* with what word of comfort
solor, ari, atus comfort, console
irascor, i I am becoming angry
sic meos amores is this (how you treat) my love?

paulum quid libet allocutionis (da mihi) give me any little bit of sympathy
maestius: comparative degree
maestus, a, um sad
lacrimis Simonideis: abl. of comparison than the tears of Simonides
Simonideus belonging to Simonides: a Greek lyric and elegiac poet (556-467 B.C.), famous in antiquity for his dirges

Martial Writes About Friends

TO SABIDIUS

non amo te, Sabidi, nec possum dicere quare:
  hoc tantum possum dicere, non amo te.

MARTIAL, *EPIGRAMS* I.32

TO FISHFACE

dicis amore tui bellas ardere puellas,
  qui faciem sub aqua, Sexte, natantis habes.

MARTIAL, *EPIGRAMS* II.87

TO VELOX

scribere me quereris, Velox, epigrammata longa:
  ipse nihil scribis. tu breviora facis.

MARTIAL, *EPIGRAMS* I.110

TO PONTILIANUS

cur non mitto meos tibi, Pontiliane, libellos?
  ne mihi tu mittas, Pontiliane, tuos!

MARTIAL, *EPIGRAMS* VII.3

TO THE CONNAISSEUR

tu Setina quidem semper vel Massica ponis,
  Papyle, sed rumor tam bona vina negat:
diceris hac factus caelebs quater esse lagona.
  nec puto, nec credo, Papyle, nec sitio.

MARTIAL, *EPIGRAMS* IV.69

To Sabidius
METRE: ELEGIAC COUPLET

Martial makes it clear that Sabidius is not a friend!

quare why, for what reason
tantum only

To Fishface
METRE: ELEGIAC COUPLET

If Sextus was once a friend, he will be no longer!

bellus, a, um beautiful
ardeo, ere burn

facies, ei, f face
nato, are swim

To Velox
METRE: ELEGIAC COUPLET

Martial answers one of his literary critics.

queror, eri complain
breviora = breviora epigrammata; breviora:
   comparative degree too short

To Pontilianus
METRE: ELEGIAC COUPLET

Martial writes to a contemporary poet.

libellus, i, m little book

To the Connaisseur
METRE: ELEGIAC COUPLET

Martial denies believing the rumours about his friend Papylus.

Setina, n. pl. the wines of Setia: Setia was
   a town south of Rome famous for its
   wines
vel or
Massica, n. pl. the wines of Massicus:
   Massicus was a mountain in central Italy famous for its wines
pono, ere serve

nego, are deny
caelebs, libis m widower
quater four times
hac lagona: abl. by means of this bottle
lagona, ae, f bottle
puto, are think
sitio, ire be thirsty

FRIENDS

Initial Questions

On the Death of Martial
1. What do you learn about the friendship of Pliny and Martial? about Pliny's concept of friendship?

To Fabullus
1. Write a critical appreciation of this poem in which you consider (a) the effectiveness of the comic devices Catullus uses and (b) whether the poem is anything more than a joke.

To Cicero
1. How does Catullus' wit enhance an ordinary thank-you note?

To Veranius
1. This poem has been criticized as being "unpoetical." How does Catullus deliberately use this feature to produce an effect that is both natural and exuberant—an effect quite appropriate with a cry of welcome?

To Cornificius
1. What effect has the final image on the poem as a whole?

Martial Writes About Friends
1. Examine the selections by Martial in this section. What faults does Martial criticize? What is your attitude to the people in these poems? Study each poem to see how Martial achieves such reader response.

Discussion Questions

1. According to Pliny, what qualities did Martial display in his epigrams? Using the Martial selections in this section, consider the extent to which you agree with Pliny's assessment of Martial. Pliny mentions a small poem that Martial had written about Pliny. How do you think such a poem might compare with those in this section?
2. Using the four Catullan poems in this section, what do you learn about Catullus' expectations of his friends? about his own contributions to the friendships?
3. Which of the three writers in this section (Pliny, Catullus, and Martial) do you think displays the most genuine sense of friendship? Which do you feel you would want as a friend? Explain your answer.

Further Reading

Catullus, unable to sleep after a stimulating meeting with Licinius, writes a poem to his friend and fellow poet: Catullus, *Carmina* 50.

Marcus Tullius Cicero, Quintus (his brother), and Quintus (his son) write expressing their anxiety on hearing of the illness of Tiro (Cicero's freedman and secretary): Cicero, *ad Familiares* XVI.4.

Horace composes an ode praising a special wine worthy of celebrating the visit of a friend: Horace, *Odes* III.21.

Pliny writes to tell Marcellinus of the untimely death of twelve-year-old Minicia Marcella, the daughter of a mutual friend: Pliny, *Epistulae* V.16.

Vergil describes the moving and tragic story of the friendship of Nisus and Euryalus: Vergil, *Aeneid* V.315ff; IX.176ff.

PLACES

Wall painting of Harbour scene. (Naples, Naples National Museum)

SIRMIO

paene insularum, Sirmio, insularumque
ocelle, quascumque in liquentibus stagnis
marique vasto fert uterque Neptunus,
quam te libenter quamque laetus inviso,
vix mi ipse credens Thuniam atque Bithunos 5
liquisse campos et videre te in tuto.
o quid solutis est beatius curis,
cum mens onus reponit, ac peregrino
labore fessi venimus larem ad nostrum,
desideratoque acquiescimus lecto?   10
hoc est quod unum est pro laboribus tantis.
salve, o venusta Sirmio, atque ero gaude
gaudente, vosque, o Lydiae lacus undae,
ridete quidquid est domi cachinnorum.

        CATULLUS, *CARMINA* 31

Sirmio

METRE: CHOLIAMBIC

Sirmio, a peninsula jutting into Lake Garda in northern Italy, was Catullus' home. In this poem, he celebrates his return from service on the governor's staff in the Roman province of Bithynia (in modern Turkey) in Asia Minor.

paene insularum   of peninsulas

ocellus, i, m: affectionate diminutive   little eye; Tr. "gem, jewel"

quicumque, quaecumque, quodcumque   whatever, every one that

liquens, entis   liquid, clear

stagnum, i, n   pool, lake

mare, is, n   sea

uterque Neptunus   each Neptune (i.e., as god of the open sea, *mari vasto*, and of fresh water lakes, *liquentibus stagnis*)

quam libenter   with what pleasure, how gladly

inviso, ere   visit, see

5 *vix*   scarcely, hardly

mi = mihi

Thuniam atque Bithunos campos   Bithunia, a Roman province in Asia Minor, and its plains: the Thuni and the Bithuni were the two tribes that peopled Bithynia

linquo, ere, liqui   leave

campus, i, m   plain, field

tutus, a, um   safe, out of danger

solutis curis: abl. of comparison   than cares put aside

solutus, a, um   relaxed, removed

beatus, a, um   happy

repono, ere   put down

peregrinus, a, um   foreign, far-off

lar, laris, m   household god, hearth, home

10 *desidero, are, avi, atus*   desire, long for

acquiesco, ere   rest

lectus, i, m   couch, bed

quod unum est pro   the one thing that is worth, the one thing that compensates for

salve: Catullus uses the greeting usually used to address a person

venustus, a, um   charming, lovely, gracious: an attribute, usually applied to persons, greatly valued by Catullus' circle of friends

erus, i, m   master

gaudeo, ere   rejoice

Lydiae   Etruscan: the Etruscans were thought to have originally settled this area in Italy from Lydia, in modern Turkey

lacus, us, m   lake

quidquid   whatever

cachinnus, i, m   laughter

ridete...cachinnorum   laugh with as much laughter as you have

O FONS BANDUSIAE

o fons Bandusiae, splendidior vitro,
dulci digne mero non sine floribus,
   cras donaberis haedo
      cui frons turgida cornibus
primis et venerem et proelia destinat; 5
frustra: nam gelidos inficiet tibi
   rubro sanguine rivos
      lascivi suboles gregis.
te flagrantis atrox hora Caniculae
nescit tangere, tu frigus amabile   10
   fessis vomere tauris
      praebes et pecori vago.
fies nobilium tu quoque fontium,
me dicente cavis impositam ilicem
   saxis, unde loquaces   15
      lymphae desiliunt tuae.

HORACE, ODES III.13

o fons Bandusiae

METRE: FOURTH ASCLEPIAD

Horace's estate in the Sabine Hills, north of Rome, was one of his favourite retreats. It is believed that Horace named the spring near his Sabine Farm after the famous Bandusian Spring near his birthplace at Venusia in southeast Italy. In this poem, Horace praises the spring and promises to immortalize it.

fons, fontis, m spring, clear water
splendidus, a, um clear, bright
vitro: abl. of comparison than glass
vitrum, i, n glass
dignus, a, um + abl. worthy of
merum, i, n pure wine
haedus, i, m a kid, young goat
cui frons whose forehead
turgidus, a, um swelling
cornu, us, n horn
5 *venus, eris, f* love
proelium, i, n battle
destino, are foretell, predict
gelidus, a, um icy
inficio, ere dye, stain
ruber, bra, brum red
sanguis, inis, m blood
rivus, i, m stream
lascivus, a, um playful
suboles, is, f offspring
grex, gregis, m flock, herd
flagrans, antis blazing, burning
atrox, atrocis terrible, cruel
Canicula, ae, f Dog-star (*i.e.*, Sirius, in the constellation of Canis Maior, the brightest of all stars and associated by the Romans with the Dog-days—the extremely hot days of July)

10 *tango, ere* touch
frigus, oris, n coolness
amabilis, e pleasing, lovely
vomer, eris, m plough, ploughshare
taurus, i, m bull
praebeo, ere supply, furnish
pecus, oris, n herd, flock
vagus, a, um wandering
fies: fut. indic. of fio, fieri you will become
nobilis, e famous
nobilium fontium: Horace hopes this poem will make his Bandusian Spring as famous in the Roman world as others, such as the Castalian Spring at Delphi in Greece, already are
me dicente: abl. abs. when I sing of
cavus, a, um hollow
impono, ere, posui, positus place on
ilex, icis, f holm-oak
15 *saxum, i, n* rock
loquax, loquacis babbling, talkative
lympha, ae, f water
desilio, ire leap down

CICERO'S VILLA AT ASTURA

CICERO ATTICO SAL.

nihil hac solitudine iucundius, nisi paulum interpellasset Amyntae filius. cetera noli putare amabiliora
fieri posse villa, litore, prospectu maris, tumulis, his
rebus omnibus. sed neque haec digna longioribus lit- 5
teris nec erat, quod scriberem, et somnus urgebat.

CICERO, *AD ATTICUM* XII.9

MARTIAL VISITS HIS FARM

quid mihi reddat ager quaeris, Line, Nomentanus?
  hoc mihi reddit ager: te, Line, non video.

MARTIAL, *EPIGRAMS* II.38

Cicero's Villa at Astura

In this part of a letter to his friend Atticus, Cicero extols the virtues of his villa at Astura, a town near Rome, which offers solitude (sometimes) and a view of the sea.

---

sal. = *salutem dat* sends greetings

solitudine: abl. of comparison than solitude

solitudo, inis, f solitude

iucundus, a, um pleasing, pleasant; *iucundius:*
  comparative degree

paulum a little, occasionally

interpellasset = *interpellavisset; interpello,*
  are interrupt, disturb

cetera everything else

puto, are think, consider

amabilis, e amiable, lovable

fio, fieri be, become

villa, litore, prospectu, tumulis, his rebus omnibus:

abl. of comparison than the villa, the shore,
  etc.

litus, oris, n shore

prospectus, us, m. view, prospect

tumulus, i, m mound, hill

5 *dignus, a, um* + *abl.* worthy of

erat = *est:* it was the Roman custom to regard
  time from the point of view of the
  receiver of the letter

quod scriberem: rel. cl. of purpose Tr.
  "anything else to write"

urgeo, ere hang heavy over

Martial Visits His Farm

METRE: ELEGIAC COUPLET

Martial, too, enjoys a retreat to the country.

---

reddo, ere offer, give

ager, agri, m farm

quaero, ere ask

Nomentanus, a, um at Nomentum (outside
  Rome)

PLACES

Initial Questions

Sirmio

1. How does Catullus re-create his feelings of joy and pleasure on returning home? Collect the examples of the personification of Sirmio. What does such humanization of Sirmio contribute to Catullus' communication of joy? How do Catullus' phrases describing his year abroad contribute to his expression of his feelings at homecoming?

o fons Bandusiae

1. Horace is a master of creating visual word pictures. Examine the poetic elements that result in the image of the kid and of the spring. What do such visual pictures contribute to the theme of the poem? How does the description of the sacrifice affect you? What does the sacrifice add to Horace's expression of pleasure in the spring?

Cicero's Villa at Astura

1. What does Cicero appreciate about his retreat in the country? What does the ending of Cicero's letter seem to imply about Cicero's attitude to nature?

Martial Visits His Farm

1. What problem do Cicero and Martial share? How successful is each in avoiding the problem by going to a country villa?

Discussion Questions

1. Compare the extent to which each writer in this section gives a clear picture of the place he describes. Compare the extent to which each writer uses sound effects. In your opinion, which writer seems to feel most affinity for the place he writes about? Explain your answer.

Further Reading

Catullus expresses his joy at setting out from Bithynia: Catullus, *Carmina* 46.
Cicero explains to Atticus why he likes to visit his birthplace, Arpinum, as frequently as possible: Cicero, *de Legibus* II.2-3.
Horace praises the simplicity of country living: Horace, *Epodes* 2.